I want to REMEMBER *this*

RUMI TSUCHIHASHI

I WANT TO
REMEMBER THIS

SEATTLE, WA

Rumi Tsuchihashi/Inside Out Living Books
hello@rumitsuchihashi.com

I Want to Remember This / Rumi Tsuchihashi. —1st ed.
ISBN 9781088005088

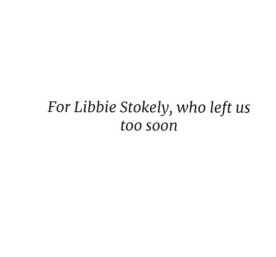

*For Libbie Stokely, who left us
too soon*

Contents.

I keep forgetting what's really important.

T his is an unpleasant thought that comes to me regularly.

All day long, my mind is full of so many things to do and remember. *I must remember to email so-and-so about such-and-such. I must remember to reschedule next week's carpool. I must remember to update my auto insurance policy before the due date.*

So many things to remember. Yet, ultimately, are these the things that really matter?

My heart says, "Not really."

Does this sound familiar?

Once, I got huffy and asked myself, "Why is remembering what matters so hard?"—in a rather demanding tone. I waited for an answer. No answer came. But I did get something: an urge to make a list.

In the following pages are some of the ideas and bits of memories that turned up when I reflected on what I don't ever want to forget. Some of these memories are big moments in my life, and some are tiny little things. Each one feels precious and important, sometimes for reasons I can't even explain.

Maybe explaining "why" it's important isn't the point. Maybe the point is simply remembering.

My hope is that this book will inspire you to make your own list, too—a list of the things *you* want to remember.

The highlights of your life. The moments that feel especially tender, moving, significant, or beautiful to you.

Your list might have three items or perhaps hundreds, and the length doesn't matter. The act of writing it out may help you remember things you'd nearly forgotten.

What do you want to remember from your life, most of all?

Here is what I want to remember from mine.

Belly Dance.

"*O*baachan, pat your tummy!" I'd say, looking up hopefully at my grandma.

She'd oblige, every time.

And I would fill my eardrums with my own squeals of delight as her belly jiggled.

Calling, calling.

I like shopping with my mother. Whenever I'm trying to choose between two nearly identical things, she'll ask, "Which one is calling to you?"

And with that invitation, I'm able to quiet my pros-and-cons-list-making brain, and tune into my heart and belly instead. Sometimes the answer comes in an instant, other times it takes a minute.

But I hear the calling, and I can finish buying, free of any regret.

Grief spasms.

My friend—we'll call her Rose—taught me this term one spring afternoon. We were seated on the rooftop deck of a chic Korean restaurant: two polished professionals, enjoying well-deserved happy hour cocktails.

Grief is more spontaneous than linear, Rose said of her divorce experience as she set down her glass. I was in the early stages of my own divorce then. I felt for her pain and nodded vigorously as she laid out the details of her more harrowing moments.

"That sounds so hard, and it makes so much sense," I said, while hiding the touch of cringe I felt inside.

One Thursday evening soon after, I was skipping down the aisles of Costco, pushing a giant, grocery-and-toilet-paper-filled cart, on a mission to find electric toothbrush heads.

Then, voila! I spontaneously transformed into a loud, trembling, tear-and-snot-gushing machine, frozen in place for all the other shoppers to see.

"Grief is like that," said a voice in my head, sounding just like Rose.

Envy.

I want to be that person who's fully in touch with the wide-eyed wonder about the world they had when they were four years old— at age 24, 54, or 104.

Having it all.

Is the feeling of his arm wrapped around my waist, the cat nestling into my chest, all of us sleeping as three nesting spoons.

Question for you.

One fall evening, I was sitting on a creaky old metal folding chair in a church basement with about fifty other adults. Onstage was a parent educator. About halfway through her talk, she touched on what courage means to her. This is how she defined the word for us.

"Courage is taking a step in the direction of what you know to be right, when it'd be so much easier not to."

She repeated herself. Which was good, because what she was saying was news to me and I needed to hear it again.

Until that evening, I'd thought of courage as a trait akin to good eyesight (which I don't have) or towering height (which I also don't have).

Until that evening, I'd thought courage was something that the people who are blessed with it use with theatrical flair—so "the others" like me can watch and applaud them from our seats.

Until that evening, I hadn't known that courage was an action and an everyday choice available to everyone. Even to, yes, me.

It was great to learn that I'd been mistaken.

But with this great knowledge came great responsibility to ask myself,

"What feels right? And what's a step in that direction that I'd rather not take because it'd be easier not to?"

And nothing was ever the same again after those questions had been asked.

Wait a minute.

I can feel judged, insecure, whatever, and let that feeling be for a minute without rushing to fix or fight it.

Unbelievable.

Do you know how strong a day-old infant's grip is? I swear, if they were holding onto a line in that tiny hand, they could tow a 3-ton pickup truck.

Maybe.

If I feel as though I don't have a lot to show for my life at this moment, maybe that's because my story isn't over yet.

If someone else's life looks wonderfully accomplished or "successful" at this moment, maybe that story will stay. But maybe something will change tomorrow. Maybe their life also looks the way it does because the story isn't over yet.

It's a good idea not to judge the worth of a human life by its appearance in the moment.

TEN

The Special Spot by the kitchen door.

The first time I sat there was a Wednesday at 2:08 a.m. and he still wasn't home.

Then, about three years later, my son asked, "Why do you like that spot?" Without realizing it, I'd made a nightly habit of resting on that same square of ceramic tile, leaning on the pantry door to read on my phone.

So that's where I was one pitch dark Monday evening, when another he called to say, "I think I'm falling in love with you."

The original Special Spot.

The Beverly Cleary section of the school library. Every indoor recess, I'd set my butt down there, alone. I can still feel the scratchy carpet under my crisscrossed legs. I can still hear my own muffled and mock-horrified gasps at Ramona's latest antics.

Permission granted.

It's okay not to be okay. It's okay not to be okay. It's okay not to be okay. It is truly, truly okay not to be okay.

Crossing the divide.

Three-and-a-half-year-old me
didn't want to be next to
Ojiichan at that busy
intersection in Victoria, B.C.
We'd been apart for a year, and now
grandpa smelled funny, so I inched
away.

But when my right foot landed on the
street too soon, it was his hand that
firmly enveloped mine. He didn't
yank or yell at me. He didn't even
gasp.

When I looked up at him seconds
later, *Ojiichan* returned a soft gaze
through his black-rimmed glasses.

And soon a warm, liquidy tingle
sprang from where our palms
touched.

This feels like love, I thought much
later.

FOURTEEN

$25.

I lifted that check above my head and up to the light. I'd sold my first piece of writing, and this was proof.

In that moment if my chest could talk, it would've said, "Hooray! I can't believe it!"

And if my fingers could talk, they would've said, "Well, I believe it."

When a long-imagined scene becomes reality through effort and opportunity, the result feels magi-logical.

Lexical-gustatory synesthesia.

The juicy insides of a ripe tomato, picked fresh off the vine in late summer, is what the sun tastes like.

Live. Laugh. Love.

I knew this would be the last time I saw her alive. And yet, my eyes were glued to the dumb variety show streaming from a mint-green cube of a TV on my dearest grandma's bedside.

There were contestants dressed in puffy insect costumes. One after another, they attempted to walk across water by traversing barely inflated plastic leaves. I couldn't contain my giggles when their epic fails predictably followed.

I've spent many years feeling horrible about how this scene played out, fixating on my bad granddaughter-ness and how I could've, should've behaved differently in those crucial last moments we had together. But suddenly, in my 20,247th replay I see something new.

Where there is life and pure love between people, laughter will enter.

And so, it did. Even in a hospital room for the dying.

SEVENTEEN

Be humble, be great.

We'd been having one of those conversations, the kind that makes you feel like you're parting clouds with your collective breaths.

All the confusion from an hour ago? Faded. All the loneliness and disconnection I was suffering from for weeks on end? A distant memory. Sitting quietly beside my friend in that hot tub, I was now one with the bubbling warm water, with the sky at dusk, with the squawking crows in the distance, and with the all-knowing one.

My friend broke the silence. "Well, you know what that wise person I know said," giving me a wink and then quoting said person.

"Wow, that is so spot on," I replied. But I didn't know who this wise person was. So I asked sheepishly for their identity, intent on searing it into my brain forever.

He said, "You did, dumbass."

Let it stand.

Say, "I'm sorry" and do not give explanations or excuses afterwards.

Heaven on Earth.

If that were the name of a perfume, it'd smell of your lover, that tucked away spot on the neck, just below the chin.

Just, don't.

His large blue eyes blazed with confidence. Our boss, and just about everyone else in the department, showered praise on him. He had a Harvard degree. He spoke Japanese and Mandarin with ease, and he'd flash a brilliant, white-toothed smile with every pause in his speech.

And this guy, upon 1) noticing me in the hallway (!!!) and 2) learning that I'd never colored my hair in my then 23 years on the planet, offered to perform the dye job Saturday afternoon, in his own bathroom, with his own two hands. "You would look amazing," he said.

Two Saturdays later, I was in my bathroom, alone and naked from the waist up, using my own two hands to fix the burnt orange frizzy mess. (Many more fix-it jobs followed.)

Note: Don't use your tresses, or any other body part, to buy attention, adoration, or admiration from someone—or from a group of folks— who wouldn't give those things to you just as you are.

TWENTY-ONE

My 7-day feel-better recipe.

I like challenges. The kind that involve a specific activity and happen over a set number of days. These challenges are especially helpful when I feel "all over the place" inside. I've tried many versions made by others and loved them. My self-imposed, 7-day version, however, goes like this.

1. Own the feeling.
2. Find at least one kind and encouraging friend and tell them about it.
3. Come up with one small, life-giving thing to do every day.

A too-easy action is just
about right.

4. Pick the daily amount of time
   you can give to this small
   thing. Then cut the time in
   half. (In the past, I've gone
   from committing one-
   minute to 30 seconds.)

5. Do the thing. Share the
   "wins" with those kind and
   encouraging friends of
   yours.

6. Rinse and repeat until day
   seven. Forget a day along the
   way? Forgive and move onto
   the next day.

7. Celebrate!

Challenges are fun and invigorating. I
highly recommend you try it next
time you need a boost.

P.S. What does it mean to feel "all
over the place"?

For me, the feeling is most often produced by a mix of juggling, spreading myself thin, and leaving a trail of loose ends behind—in other words, after trying (too hard) to give, give, give, and still have it together.

Long ago, something in the water taught me that behaving that way—and feeling perennially anxious that I'm failing to meet expectations—was a sort of "existential woman tax" I owed.

For a good portion of my life, I've responded to being anxious by trying harder and harder still to be "good."

Initiating a challenge is my way of hitting pause to that cycle. It's a chance to say no to that be-everything-to-everyone expectation and be nowhere but right here—for myself—if only for a week, and for 30-seconds a day.

Once upon a time.

I flew a Goodyear blimp over the rolling green hills of Auburn, Washington. True story.

Try being hopeless instead.

I was in a shitty situation with someone. Shit had gotten shittier still, and I was telling this wise friend all about it. "I'm so sorry, Rumi," she said, folding her hands into her lap. "It's hopeless, isn't it?"

I curled my lips and nodded appreciatively, mouthing "yes, yes" without sound. But inside my head, the words were roaring.

Wait, what? Hopeless?
What's she talking about? Isn't
hopelessness the same thing as giving
up?

Hope is good. Surely, I can do better than call things hopeless, right? Dammit, I need hope...

Then a thud in my chest interrupted my mental monologue.

It's so easy to say "I need hope" when I really mean: "I'm bitter. The situation and the other person are wrong, and what's wrong needs correcting. And I will make things right."

If I skip over acceptance of what is, then it's not hope I'm holding onto. It's denial.

When my response to her, "Yes, it's hopeless," finally came out loud, the words tasted pretty sweet.

TWENTY-FOUR

West Side story.

One August day, I got an idea. "Enough with the gross and stuffy A train!" I said. "Today, Imma bike to work instead!"

Never mind that I'm uncoordinated. Or that I'd be cycling almost the entire length of Manhattan— alongside *very* busy, unfamiliar roads. Once the idea took hold it wouldn't let go.

So off I went on two wheels to Riverside Drive.

My hands shook a bit at first. I felt queasy. But before long, I started hearing the hum of my whirling wheels meld with engine noise, construction sounds, and babies' cries. I smelled sweat and hot dogs in the wind grazing my face.

I had some close calls, but I also had momentum to keep me going.

By the time I made it near the Chelsea Piers, my whole world felt sparkly. Even the drunk men I had to swerve around looked like they were covered in fairy dust.

With every push of the pedal, I marveled at how far my own two feet could take me. (And yes, I made it safely to the West Village.)

Whenever I think back to a time when I felt intensely alive, I return to this scene.

And I get curious: why, in everyday life, is it so hard to feel life force pulsating through my veins as I did then?

After all, all it took that day was being open to a different way to get to work.

TWENTY-FIVE

Unbroken.

If you're reading this, you've so far survived every test, every heartbreak, every move, every mean person, every blunder, every missed deadline or late arrival, every sharp word that wounded you, every important thing you've ever broken or misplaced, every loss of a loved one, every questionable decision, every time you got caught doing something bad, every act of violence inflicted on you, every inopportune loss of body function, every injustice, and every weather, financial, traffic, familial or health (near) disaster.

Whew. What a feat.

TWENTY-SIX

What's your secret?

That morning, the last of the golden ginkgo leaves were falling, leaving the branches bare. The air was still; and the pond, a crystalline mirror of the blue sky and the frosted pine needles hovering above it.

"Why is the garden so beautiful this time of year?" I said, not really expecting an answer from the person beside me. He, a seven-foot-tall, red-haired former Buddhist monk, and a regular Seattle Japanese Garden visitor, bent down to answer me. "It's because the most exquisite beauty lives in close proximity to death," he said.

He continued talking after pausing to study my scrunched-up forehead.

"And if you can inhabit that same space, people will be drawn to you without knowing why. They'll ask you, over and over again, 'What's your secret?'"

TWENTY-SEVEN

Mantra of the year, and possibly for all the years to come.

All that you need, you already have.

What do you want to remember? Jot down whatever comes to mind.

_____

_____

_____

_____

_____

Acknowledgments.

Thank you, Cat, David, Lacey, Lisa, Jen, Julie, Marian, Mary Anne, Julie, Peg, Roberta, Teri Jo, Terrace, Tom, and Ursula, for keeping the faith through my ups and downs and inspiring me with your awesomeness.

Thank you, Kai and Reina. I might be your mom, but you raised me up. I've had this dream to write a book since before you were born, but I needed to grow up to make it come true.

Thank you, Pete, for loving me every day. And for all the other things. You are immense.

Thank you, Libbie. I didn't know it then, but my writing was with you in your last hours on this earth. Whenever I feel like giving up on writing, I think of you and wonder what you'd say to me.

Thank you, Claudia, for carefully reading through this manuscript so I could present it in the best light.

And dear reader, thank you for going on this journey with me. Your company means everything.

ABOUT THE AUTHOR

Rumi Tsuchihashi is based in Seattle, Washington, and works in marketing and communications. She loves helping people take what's inside of them and bring it out with words and images. She also loves to eat, visit family in Tokyo, put bow ties on her cat, and smell salt air. *I Want To Remember This* is her first book. You can find more of her writing at rumitsuchihashi.com.